The John Chronicles

Making Peace With Mania

Kalvin Seth Brubaker

All illustrations by Ambrus Diossy, used by permission.
Cover- “Mare Nostrum”

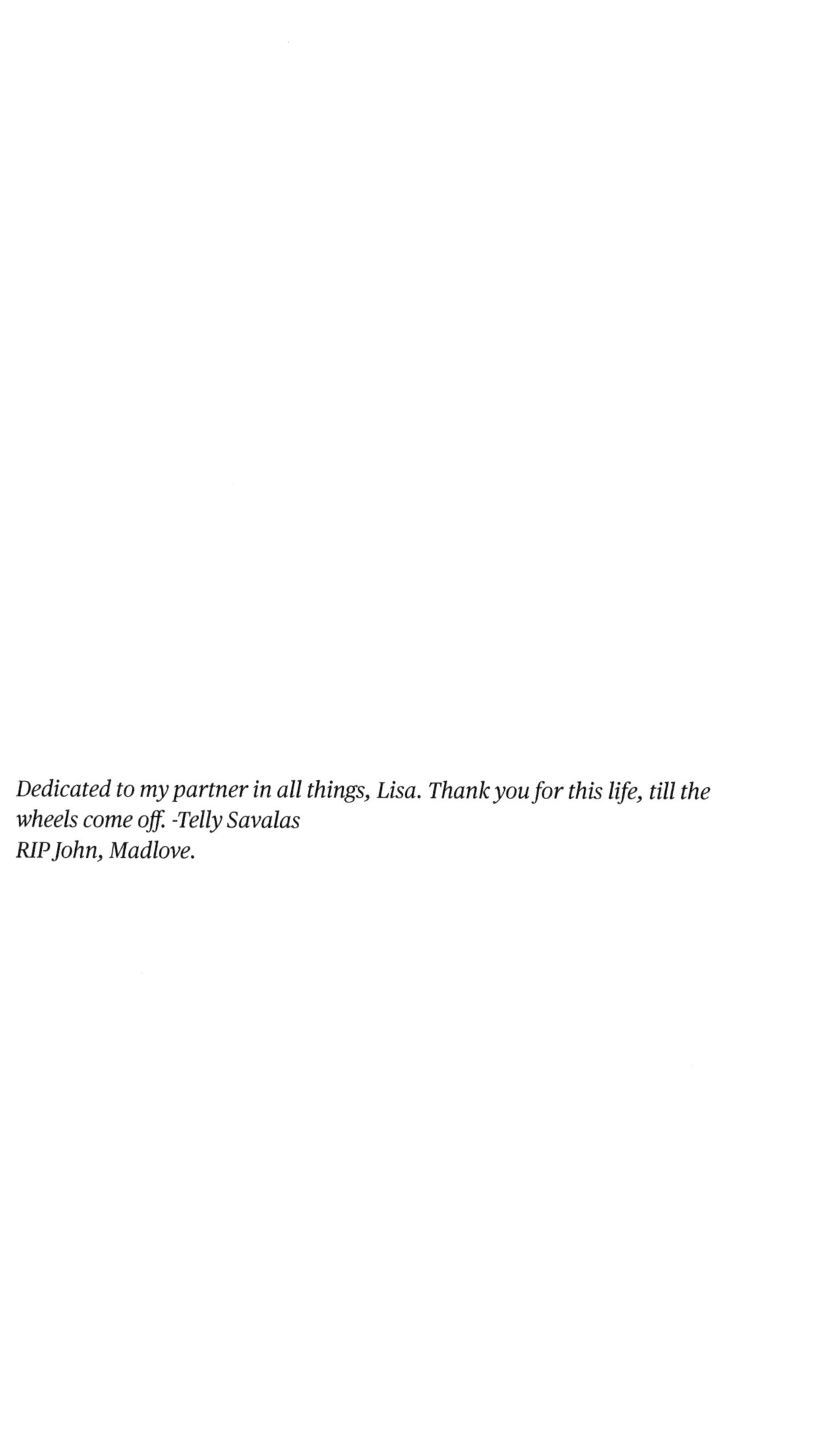

Dedicated to my partner in all things, Lisa. Thank you for this life, till the wheels come off. -Telly Savalas
RIP John, Madlove.

Prologue

When I got the call that John had died it didn't surprise me in the least, to be selfishly honest it was a relief. Who he had become in later years was immaterial. What was of importance is what he had been to me; he'd been a star. Bright, warm and magnetically heavy he pulled me into his orbit as part of the set when I met him in High School. Then later he appeared like a shamanic guide when I was navigating the tempests of mental instability, identity and life choices.

As I reminisced about who he was and went through the stages of communally mourning him with old friends, I had the experience of thoroughly revisiting my memories. What I found was a powerful maxim. For what I realized is that if you enter into the annals of your past in brutal earnestness, details emerge to shine a light on the heavily biased stories you've repeated to yourself about yourself. We constantly create a narrative that rationalizes our actions, placing blame elsewhere and glorifying our role. Everyone tends to paint themselves to be either the hero or the victim (or heroic victim) in their version of the account but when you truly inspect the case file with more mature eyes (peeled for your ego's tells) you see the discrepancies.

I got extremely lucky. I found a partner in life who's sheer will and tenacity were sufficient to hold me accountable to address and process the suppressed emotional energy that drove my self destructive patterns. More importantly though I made the decision to actually do the work rather than run away from or mask/self-medicate my way through it. It's constant. It's difficult but commensurately rewarding.

John had different demons. Bigger, scarier and deeper in his foundation that he continually added to. He either never got the chance or never had the right motivation to go into where they lived and confront them. Perhaps in the next life.

There are keystones in your timeline, moments that coalesce all that came before and change everything after. That is what mania did for me, and twice in four years that storm picked me up and deposited me somewhere else.

"You're only given a little spark of madness. You mustn't lose it."-Robin Williams

"The Tempest"- Ambrus Diossy.

1 “NYC- ‘It’s not me, it’s you’.”

The problem with tolerances is in the calibration. What may very well work for a time is subject to constant change. Manipulating your energies/dynamic mood swings seems easy enough to accomplish (chemically or otherwise) but you’re usually out in front of the emotional hangover, not privy to all the eventualities you’ve created. Until there is a correction.

"SLEEP, THOSE LITTLE SLICES OF DEATH; OH HOW I LOATHE THEM." EDGAR ALLAN POE

Falling into mania is a vertically integrated affair. Brain activity increases, momentum manifests both physically and emotionally rendering sleep unobtainable. Sleep deprivation acts like its own drug, sharpening visceral responses and generating more brain activity. This loop repeats exponentially and is exacerbated by any attempt to self medicate.

So very quickly this spinning action is reacted to by all the systems around you in the form of rejection. It's an inherently human impulse to get away from "crazy".

Fired, evicted and dumped within a very short span of time with no savings, credit or tangible support feels like persecution. Delusions are famously fluid for their ability to reinforce themselves. Once the idea sets in of a conspiracy moving against you, all other sources to the contrary become suspect.

There was a classic arcade video game called Asteroids. Where you piloted a ship in space around a field of moving rocks and you could either shoot them or maneuver yourself away or if you were stuck in a position where there was no escape possible you could use the "Hyperspace" button which would magically wormhole you to another random spot in the space. The problem was that the area you were transported to might be even worse than the one you were initially in. Mania was my hyperspace button; the life I had been able to haphazardly piece together in NYC had very little margin for error and now that my overstuffed emotional energy storage area had been released I was spiraling. Getting bounced all the way down to where crazy seems to be gravitationally drawn to on the corner edge of the map like detritus swirling in an immense national draining ditch, Florida.

Flori-duh, God's Waiting Room, Home of the Newly Wed and the Nearly Dead, so far south it's actually part of NY, The Hollywood of South America, a place where humidity and in-breeding have harbored radical ignorance since the Civil War, a playground for the wealthy, the highest alcohol and drug consumption anywhere in America and somehow it always seems to be the deciding vote in Presidential elections. I'd successfully escaped here once before and for my sins I was back.

"Oceanus Procellarum" by Ambrus Diossy.

2. County

Blur, movement, images, pain and a violent awakening already in motion like playing a sport in a dream when the alarm goes off. I came to, up and out of the vision of a war movie where I'd been gassed in battle to realize I was outside, facedown thrashing against the dirt and leaves, handcuffed naked, my face on fire with pepper spray.

Delusional and heavily self medicated on top of the cumulative effects of three weeks of profound sleep deficit (able to drift off 15 min max) I found myself injured and facing multiple felonies in the Indian River County Jail.

First the Infirmary cell for Christmas Day where the overhead lights stayed on continually and a tv out of reach played the film "A Christmas Story" on a loop for 24hrs straight without reprieve. Then giving way to weeks in a "Birdcage"- a psychiatric eval solitary cell with a small window into the adjoining pod where I could entertain myself by periodically screaming murderous obscenities at a revolving cast of inmate faces which would appear and later watch as all the pods were lead outside for rec right under me as we continued the time honored game of "You ain't Shit...Fuck you bitch...You ain't hard...I'mma fuckin kill you muthafucka".

It was sometime after I'd been granted general population residency when I volunteered to go to an AA meeting to pass the time. AA, NA and Chapel were all popular distractions, sweeping up the various career or short time derelicts into a structure rife with the promise of change and answers. Seated in a circle, busy going through the machinations of sharing, reading from the Big Book and the serenity prayer when I should look up and see a familiar face. The surreal nature of all I'd been through these past months hampered my cognition skills, I struggled to make sense of what my eyes were seeing and then fought to accurately match that image to my memory and then to this place. A fellow inmate smiled widely at me and it was like being warmed by the sun, John Fucking Miner!

I hadn't seen John since high school (I was now 24) but his goofy "aw sucks" toothy grin and crazy/ knowing eyes were a welcome sight. He had been arrested for assaulting his younger brother who he'd told me wouldn't stop knocking on the bathroom door while John was trying to enjoy shooting some Dilaudid. I told him all about my charges, how I would finally get to see a judge soon (after waiting 90 days) and that my public defender thought I would be sent to a six month rebab facility in Jensen Beach called C.A.R.P. This inspired him and he vowed to follow me there.

"Mercury" detail- Ambrus Diossy

3. C.A.R.P.

Jensen Beach, FL. A hundred and twenty crackheads,
one pill popper lady who stole a doctor's script pad and me

all sequestered in a former motel on the shores of the Indian River in a private rehab program whose roster was filled ninety-nine percent by people on probation and paid for by The Department of Corrections. Summertime in Florida is an abomination of heat and humidity which leech the energy and morale out of the best, most grounded and focused individuals- these were not those.

I'd been there a month when entered into this was the aforementioned walking dichotomy that was John Joseph Miner. Being in John's presence was like hanging with a rockstar who insisted you have more fun than you thought you could stand. He was good looking, charming as all get out and mischievous as the day is long. His mind was always churning, ruminating and calculating how to make the absolute most of the people and options he could lay his hands on. He was driven (unhealthily some might say) to avoid anything he deemed boring. He had come from money and could naturally fit in with all races, classes, crowds and cliques. He was unafraid, unapologetic and a master of creating the world around him to suit his whims.

I remember once in high school we'd gone out west of town trespassing skillfully in cow country to pick magic mushrooms. We'd filled half a hefty bag full and processed the haul expertly at my house to produce an extremely concentrated, deceptively sweet tea. We'd done this dozens of times and the confidence and glee we all felt performing this ritual was like an excited dance. We measured out double shots for our band of freaks (at this concentration, one ounce would propel you for hours once it kicked in) and set off driving to a house party with the fancy private school kids on the beachside. Once there, John proclaimed to the party that the gallon jug he brought was moonshine tea and the trendy rich kids passed it around greedily. The vibe and momentum of it all had me initially onboard, but when I took John aside and said I thought we should tell these kids what's about to happen he got dark. He was like a petulant child and I was fucking up his elaborately planned and executed fun. He made overtures to lessen and rationalize what it was he was doing but I could sense there was real menace and sadism in his eyes. He had chaos in him and he wanted others to share it. I would later come to find out that he had been damaged at a young age by an adult family friend, that he'd exposed the abuse to both families and that it had been basically ignored and covered up. I can't imagine the concentric circles of emotional pain that caused him.

John and I stuck close at C.A.R.P., it was a six month program, the first eight weeks of which you were confined to the property and intensive AA style meetings/activities all day. You could get a menial job after that and continue meetings at night. We talked a lot about what led us both to being here (this was already John's eighth rehab) he was well schooled in the themes, culture and literature. Through our conversations he was the first person who concluded that what I had in fact experienced was a manic, Bi-Polar event. This was the first I'd heard of the condition outside of Jimi Hendrix's song "Manic-Depression". He'd had similar manifestations albeit with different specifics, he was what's known as "dual diagnosis", where there's a pronounced mental condition that's married to substance abuse. We talked all about possible plans we had for when we got out, adventures and cities we felt drawn to, ways in which we could make a big splash, etc. He lasted a month. He flashed his penis at one of the former self described crack whores, she told on him and he was sent packing.

I said and did all the right things to complete C.A.R.P.-

I resumed my life, albeit encumbered now with 3 years of probation to serve and restricted from residing anywhere but Flori-duh. I truly wish I had more to show for my time spent there but I was still woefully and selfishly self medicating and tunnel visioned about the goal of finishing probation and getting the fuck outta Florida.

Right before my escape plans could unfold I fell madly in love with another Old Soul light worker who was cycling through her own dalliances with self medication. Sarah was 8 years younger than me and shined like the sun. I eventually (of course) disappointed, confounded and embarrassed her enough that she had to let me go, so sorry about that Sarah you deserved ever so much better.

"Bermuda"-Ambus Diossy.

4. LA-

(Insert a redundant 1100 day montage of non-manic, tedious strife in the humid bubble of mundane idiocy that is Florida...)

3 Years and 3000 miles away...Manic again

Blasting back into consciousness my first thought was just how cold it gets at night in California even in Summer. The freight train of momentum in my brain picked up the narrative right where I'd left off; "I'd been racing through the ever more wild roads and paths in the hill country of what I later learned was Perris, CA out in Riverside County in the Saab my friend Chris had negotiated the sale of and subsequently floated me the money for as my cashiers' check which represented all my moving money would take some three days to clear. In my grandiose, fill in the blanks mind I had shifted from the fairly realistic impulse of driving to San Diego to visit my old friend Misty (no plan, address, experience driving on LA freeways or map) and now after an entire night of rally car-esc driving on instinct I had shifted into believing that my former elusive boss who had been using his formidable trust fund to produce movies for his actress wife was actually going to welcome me with open arms and recognize the value and genius of the film ideas I was going to pitch him(complete illusion) and now somehow I was out here in the meth producing high desert area feverishly scouting for movie locations when I launched the four door hatchback going sixty down a horse trail and bottomed out.

There's a component of my mania whereby any and all money on hand must be spent immediately, hot-potato style. I'd already burned through my debit card in the forty eight hours since taking possession of the Saab with very little to show for it. There was a complex array of maneuvers criss-crossing through greater Los Angeles involving different conspiracies and games of hanging out in hotel lobbies and hospitals taking advantage of the hospitality while interacting with various other people and "dazzling" them with my epic stories about the adventure I was on. Smoking dozens of Pall Mall straight one tens and drinking Olde English twenty two ounce malt liquors(The 40's didn't stay cold enough for my pace).

After covering the Saab with thick sheets of muddy water soaked burlap I'd found nearby (the trails appeared to have been used as high school party spots replete with all the requisite litter). In my mania there's also always an element of paranoia which feeds the alacrity of the momentum and by camouflaging the Saab I felt safer from any deep-state sponsored aerial reconnaissance. I set out on foot to try to improve my situation and get back on track as is the want of the stunning "importance" of the mission, every little thing has such gravitas and meaning when you're in it. I trekked through makeshift shooting galleries (the gunpowder kind) where I collected handfuls of spent brass casings that I used as whistles of varied pitch depending upon the caliber. It grew dry hot as sin and I found among the broken bottles used for target practice a nearly full gatorade that passed the "funky test" (my tried and true challenge to my body to consume anything which did not look, smell or taste funky). Being only a week into the sleep dep, my auditory and visual hallucinations were just starting and I welcomed them as I passed through a canyon of tall stone outcroppings which the mid morning sun animated into shadowy but approving Indian Shaman Ancestor faces. Eagles (or were those buzzards?) called out their encouragement to me as I was drawn to the top of one ridge after another until I saw the first manmade interruption in the khaki landscape, a large radar dish atop a building on the next valley over. I reveled in having a tangible goal for my quest and put my body to the test jog-traipsing over hill and dale to arrive at what turned out to be a cable television relay. Either my schtick was convincing enough or the manager just wanted me outta there but nevertheless he directed me to the sixty something year old cowboy type fella who did odd jobs (fitting for me). I got in his old 4x4 and in addition to the diarrhetic diatribe I subjected him to I was able to find the trailhead and after I got out to skip my way around and retrace my actual footprints we found the Saab. He said maybe four words in total the entire time but nodded occasionally and attached a tow rope to dislodge the stranded Saab-Turtle from it's perch. My acrobatics had ripped the muffler off so I put it in the trunk but otherwise she ran so I followed the cowboy out onto the feeder road in my now monstrously loud sounding ride, I gave him a fancy bone handled lock blade as payment which he seemed content with.

48 hours earlier. -

(So, to recap) I was fresh off three years probation which inhibited me from leaving the state of Florida...Did you know that corrections is the number four industry in Florida? Tourism first, then citrus, next is cattle, then comes the building and maintaining of the many public and private prisons and operating the probation departments around the state. "Come on vacation, leave on probation, return on violation."

It was a genuine water to wine miracle that I hadn't violated. I even had to serve a year of county probation(for a drunken Christmas party fistfight) on top of the three years state probation that I already had. Weekly calls to my PO on Mondays where three numbers had been drawn and if they matched the last digit of your DOC number you had to go provide a urinalysis.

I'd been working as a bartender at a lucrative but seasonal fine dining restaurant where the wealthy Chef/ Owner would transport and accommodate the entire back of the house and key positions up front from their Summertime Bed & Breakfast in Nantucket to their snowbird winter home in Vero Beach.

I hadn't yet learned or wasn't prepared to admit that the correlation between my alcohol/ drug intake and my precarious mental states were inextricably linked. It wasn't that I didn't care what happened to me, I had just convinced myself that I was intelligent enough to control it all. More suppression of the emotional energy and masking the roots of my problems.

I'd made plans to move out to LA at the end of the Winter season. Selling, giving or throwing away all but a few suitcases and shipping a trunk. I insisted to the dismay of the travel agent (they used to be a thing) that my ticket be one-way. "But it costs the same, why don't you get a roundtrip?" Because of the symbolism I declared. If I'd arrived in LA on a ship I would've burned it Cortez style, no going back.

Unfortunately for me, part of my conquest of LA (and the subsequent restart and success of my would-be acting career) involved acquiring a cycle of oral anabolic steroids to get that "Movie Star Physique". Well, unbeknownst to me, steroids act like mania jet fuel propellant. I was doomed to repeat a fire sale of the mind and of all material progress up till now.

My nearly ever patient, newly married friends in LA were former theater troupe members from the NYC days. It didn't take much contact with me to deduce that I was a swirling dumpster fire and they graciously parked me at an International Youth Hostel on Melrose after I'd disappeared with the newly bought used car they'd helped me find and when I reappeared I had given the car away to a family that had come to my aid after getting the car stuck on back trails during an insane scenario eighty miles away in Perris. After about a week I'd worn out the money leftover on the cashiers check after paying for the now departed Saab and also my credit and welcome at the Hostel (which I'd bullshitted my way into btw, claiming that I was a Canadian citizen, they didn't rent to Americans).

John came to my rescue, he and his new wife and baby son were living nearby in Bellflower where he was working as a union boat captain on construction ships. He knew from experience right away the nature of my condition. They took me out to eat, paid my outstanding Hostel bill, bought me a beeper and put a couple hundred bucks in my hands which he insisted was to be considered a gift. John alluded to an upcoming trip home to Florida for his wife and son and that we should go to Mexico while they were away. My incurable optimism had me believing that I'd find a restaurant job quickly and then the conquest of LA dream could continue, but of course that wasn't what happened.

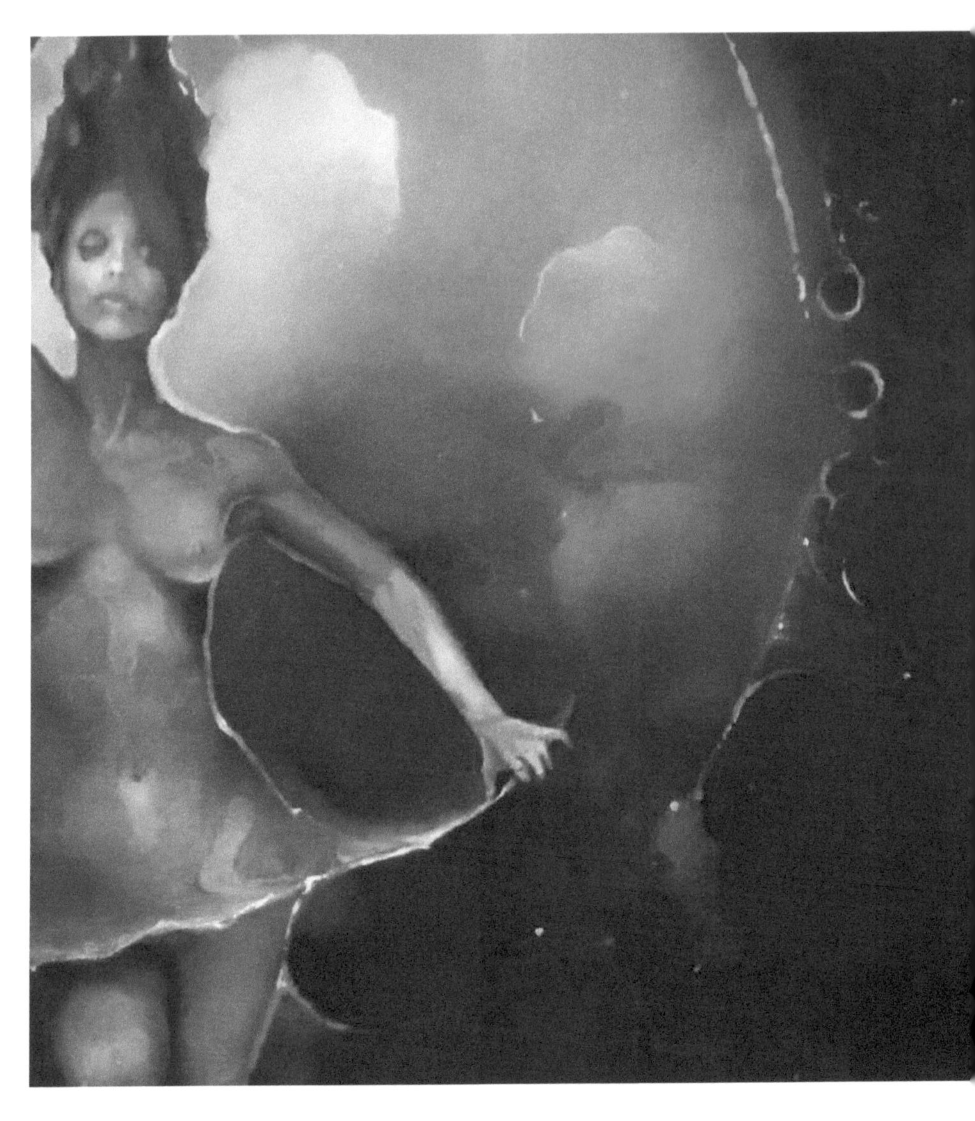

“Atomica”- Ambrus Diossy.

5. Baja

Utterly ridiculous scenarios of increasingly more elaborate and grandiose fiber came and went. Job seeking, massive planning, conspiratorial phone calls to old and new acquaintances, partying with the international Hostel clientele, drama, drinks and self harm to elicit sympathy from unwitting gay bar patrons all led to a state of zero funds or viable job prospects. I called John. He said his wife and baby had just left, he was off for four days and he had been working overtime for three months, he had two thousand dollars burning a hole in his pocket and I should get ready to go to Mexico. I sat on the patio on the Hostel, bags packed waiting for him...he was a little over twenty four hours late as the old demons of crackhouses and their lures had trapped him again temporarily. We hit the road jabbering about old times, places and people when I casually mentioned that while I was serving out my probation I was serving tables at a classic old landmark called The Ocean Grill where I waited on the wedding reception of his old ex girlfriend who'd married another of our old friends (and former crack enthusiasts) Louie. We were tooling down the I-5 going ninety as I told him and he literally had a ten minute, violent one man freak out over it. Screaming at me that I was joking, pleading that it wasn't true, mercilessly beating the steering wheel and dashboard and tearfully vowing to murder Louie and take her back, his one true love. "Hell yeah! Let's put his head on the end of a stick and swoop her up!" I offered enthusiastically... My nature is to always agree with anyone showing great emotion or authority so as to deflect that energy away from me, eventually able to gently direct it back to a better cause. I've heard this referred to as Chinese Diplomacy.

Mexico swallowed us up in its vaguely foreign aura, we drove to the outskirts of Encenada where a two bedroom villa with a kitchen, deck, your very own carport and an attached driving range where the balls were retrieved by a lone donkey pulling a hopper went for forty bucks US a night. We penetrated the port city of Encenada as day gave way. The bars gave away free tequila shots for every beer purchased and the half pack Mexican cigarettes we bought from the street carts were harsh, little and perfect at fifty cents a throw. As we walked down a side street the savvy Farmacia barker beelined right up to us as if he'd been waiting for a date and directed us inside to the counter. John stood at the well lit glass display like those kids near the candy man in the old Willy Wonka movie, pointing to whole rows of names that would take you uptown or downtown, things designed to treat anxiety , erectile dysfunction and surgical level pain. He dickered a little bit to show he was down, but paid a little over three hundred bucks for a a decent shopping bag full of little cardboard boxes with foil sheets encasing hundreds of various pills. We also picked up fruit juices and four bottles of overproof Vicario Sugar Cane liquor and retreated to the room. As I mixed up the punch in our ornate water container (don't drink the water) John decided to empty out almost all of our pill supply into a massive Molcajete (Mexican mortar & pestle used to make guacamole) smashing up the Xanax, Valium, Quaaludes, Adderall, Soma, Viagra, Dexadrine, Nembutal, Diazepam and Percosets into a big speedball dry stew. We played around with the ritualistic preparations then laid out four two foot long lines of the mixture that we snorted up like a marathon Dustbuster.

What followed was a vivid 3D montage of going back and forth to the city, strip clubs where I danced onstage with the girls while John went upstairs for his kicks, the room again and this time with some of the Americans in town for the Baja 1000, me passing out and catching glimpses of John escorting drag queen hookers in and out of the room, more more more drugs and punch till I was alone in the city and finally found a cab that brought me back to another resort next door and I had to shake the driver for the fare and double back. How long did it go on? It felt like a week but it was most likely only three days. John finally came back and announced we were outta time and money, he had a single hundred dollar bill left for gas and away we went. Within sight of the border John suddenly pulled over, he was convinced that in his fugue state he'd hidden a pack of Valium in the trunk or in the baby seat so we frantically pulled the car apart on the side of the freeway looking for any evidence that might doom us to a Mexican jail, to no avail. We breezed back into the bosom of the USA and the belly of Los Angeles, he dropped me at the Hostel and I wouldn't see him again in person for 8 years.

“Lacrimae Rerum”- Ambrus Diossy.

6. Long Beach

Much to my surprise I discovered that LA had a subway and not only that but it operated on an honor system without turnstiles, ideal for destitute manic homeless would-be actors. One of the multicolored lines took me up to Universal City where among other things I crashed an audition in the most awkward way possible and managed to steal a VHS copy of “The James Dean Story” starring a new actor I’d never heard of, James Franco. This was just the latest in the never ending series of “signs” that I was being led on the right path for a higher purpose as I had believed since age fifteen(when my father had experimented on me with his new hypnotherapy past life regression skills) that I was a reincarnation of the tragic fallen RebelGiant actor. By now I’d made my way out to Long Beach (another sign, as I’d also taken refuge on a subway train from my first manic episode in NYC with friends that put me up in Long Beach, Long Island) I was staying some nights at a Salvation Army Mission where for the price of listening to a sermon you could get a meal, a shower and a bunk for the night. There was occasionally a bit of bad noise from some of the younger ghettos boys who were convinced they had something to prove but for the most part it was just what I’d come to expect from the homeless people I’d encountered thus far. Men who'd tried. Men who were either unable or unwilling to accept the cookie cutter roles that society had allowed for them. Men with issues; dependency, education, mental stability, citizenship, opportunity, morale, motivation, momentum. They knew what steps they needed to take to get outta this lifestyle and they were either actively taking or avoiding them. LA area homeless seem like a different species from NYC- in NY you see the rind of just how fuckin hard it is to exist at all in the cramped terrarium that is NY, much less to do it without a home in that weather of extremes, unhealthy congestion and high frequency energetic buzz. By contrast, in LA you see a homeless guy lounging around his makeshift tent area on actual grass while it's seventy two and sunny and all you feel is jealous of his tan and downtime.

Occasionally citizens and criminals would cruise by the mission looking for laborers of some sort. A smooth cat who called himself Black (I told him he could call me Red) rolled up one day in his lowered four door Cadillac with Laker's flags sticking up outta the rear windows and picked me and a middle aged Mexican woman to help him effect a hustle. Simple enough, he'd had pro shoplifters pull a few bags full of random hardware pieces outta Home Depot and our job was to return all the stuff without a receipt... for cash. I was still effecting the roving movie producer persona, look and rap so I was able to get the money after I signed a sheet and showed em my ID. Not so for my Mexican lady compadre, she didn't have a cool disarming rap or US ID so she got nada. Black laughed when I told him how it went down, "You white, that's all that matters." My take was forty bucks which I quickly spent on foolishness.

Days came and went, my primary distraction was walking around following my intuition. Sometimes sleeping a few minutes here and there in the wee hours of the night at construction sites or the occasional dine and dashing (sorry Denny's-I've since always tipped 50% as penance).There were awkward dalliances with drug addicts and the lonely gay men who pursued them, heroic (in my mind) instances of unsolicited aid and a situation where I thought my heart was attacking me so I enlisted the aid of lifeguards who sent for paramedics, they quickly dismissed me after I told them that I had in fact smoked some crystal meth two days before and my vitals seemed reasonably acceptable. I'd been hanging around the mission again when two guys rolled up in vans looking to hire temp help as security for a music festival, fifty bucks for the day, the only stipulation was that you had to have khaki colored pants. I hopped to it. I forget the venue, but it was an outdoor sports complex/amphitheater and they broke us up into teams after giving us a Security T-shirt to wear. I volunteered to work at the main gate where I helped distribute the Will Call/VIP tickets and packets. The quasi famous MTV VJ Jesse Camp was my first "all access" packet recipient, and among the confusion of his film crew getting their bracelets and lanyards and the fact that he was tripping balls, I could see that he'd only need one of the many VIP access bracelets that was in his packet so I pocketed the rest. I asked to use the bathroom and cruised the concert until I saw a guy all by himself, I offered to sell him the backstage pass for forty dollars, he said ok but I had to walk him in.

I got to be friendly with one of the operators of the security company and he told me that next week they were gonna be shipping out two buses full of guards for the annual Weenie Roast festival in Irvine. The lineup was crazy; 311, Coldplay, Crazy Town, Disturbed, Jane's Addiction, Linkin Park, The Cult, Stone Temple Pilots, Blink-182 and more, I made a mental note to make sure to be there for the bus with khaki pants on.

I'd had one successful run where I'd taken a fellow mission resident, a small time swindler (he was in from Michigan and stole sunglasses from the busy shoreline tourist spots and sold em to tourists) to a Guy Fieri type loud theme bar where I gave the thick necked bartender my (now totally useless) debit card to hold for our tab as I could see where he kept the CCs and chits in little shot glasses near the register. We ran up a pretty good bill and with the dexterity of a cat I reached over and swiped my card back without anyone seeing it, then I asked to cash out. I watched with a mixture of fear and excitement as the poor frat bro rummaged around and around looking for my card, asking the other tenders, moving the register and finally giving up flustered he came back to me and said he knows he JUST saw it but he can't find my card now anywhere, did I have another one? We played it beautifully; my buddy was all bummed out, said it was his birthday and that I'd insisted he leave his money at home as tonight's festivities were on me, I of course was crushed- this was the only card I had and now I wouldn't have access to any money for my buddy's birthday dinner I wanted to buy him. The bartender felt bad, handed me fifty bucks for the trouble and said not to sweat the tab.

So the night before the Weenie roast I tried the same scam at what turned out to be a predominantly gay piano bar. The flux and flow of my energies and combination of drinks(gays tend to favor a heavy pour), sleep dep and malnourishment (I was down about forty pounds since I'd left Florida two months previous) hit me sideways and instead of trying to swipe back my flaccid debit card I made a break for it out the smoking deck through a hedge. I literally crashed into some bushes a few blocks away and slept a fitful couple hours till the sprinklers came on in the pre-dawn. Semi-refreshed but still a manic raw nerve dangling I again started the long walk to where the buses were to pick us up for Weenie Roast when I realized I wasn't wearing khakis. As I schemed en route, I nearly tripped over an old hobo in an alley. I noticed he was wearing what could be considered the remnants of khakis, I of course took this as a sign and woke him up. My pitch was jumbled as I could still feel the effects of those gay bar drinks in my system but I promised him ten bucks to swap pants with me so I could do the gig. He went for it, they fit and I told him to follow me to an ATM around the corner as I was in a hurry to catch the bus, then I just started walking faster and faster till I lost him.(hobos ain't much for cardio)

Equipped with a security shirt and after taking some slack for the state of my hobo pants(I explained that I was assigned to work in the pit and that they were gonna get ruined anyhow....*Author's Note: Never underestimate the power of a lie/explanation if you yourself can truly believe it) I bounded onto the bus. First on, last seat. I ,of course, splashed my important stories and big conspiracies to all around me, regaling my fellow low rent fake cops to all manner of gibberish on the way to the venue in Irvine. As is common in my mania, enclosed space where I have a captive audience is fraught with eventual tension. I was a lot- and talking about hard to believe shit inevitably gets called out for being the bullshit that it so clearly is. My response to this is to flash the daemon, the rage and low deep menacing animus that requires a fight or flight from any subjected to it. Nearly all in my experience except trained first responders, highly skilled martial artists, straight up Alpha thugs or other crazies choose to avert their eyes and formulate an exit strategy. About half a mile from the venue we were stuck in concert traffic, inching minimally in the rapidly rising Summer heat. Impulse control and my mania weren't on speaking terms, and I heard myself say out loud, "They need me at the concert right now, I should open that emergency exit window, jump out and run." The tall dork in the seat close to me who had earlier called me out and felt the fury, now guffawed at my proposed plan and that was all I needed. I engaged the safety handles, swung the window up and jumped out the seven feet to the hot pavement, the window crashing back down with a loud concussion but not breaking. I rolled out and started jogging alongside the bumper to bumper traffic, feeling the hot dry air in my lungs and relishing the freedom of the bus's confinement and bad juju when the positively infuriated big black bus driver rushed out the swinging doors and got in my face. I thought he was surely gonna wring my neck, spittle flying and muscles bulging as he screamed at me drill sergeant style. Mercifully he ended up just shaking his head and walking away, I trotted on to the big show.

"Neopolis"-Ambrus Diossy.

7. Irvine

The consistency and speed with which a thought becomes an idea, becomes a revelation and is then believed and embraced the complete truth while I was manic cannot be understated. Any nebulous notion could set into motion entire shifts in trajectory and the more grandiose or powerful the concept the more license it gave the delusional person(me).

So it was very quickly reported up the security chain of command about my crazy stuntmanly airborne bus exit and I was summarily ejected from the venue by a whole troupe of phony tough, hard talking minimum wage security nerds who relieved me of my company shirt. I had been given a map and a set list for the long day's event right before word of my antics had spread and as I walked through the vast sea of excited tailgaters in the massive parking lot waiting to get in I lamented to a big bunch of party people, look what "The Man" had done to me (meaning the firing and de-shirting). They took me in and offered me one of their pre-game beers, which they had a ridiculous amount of and seemed to be in a race to finish before going in and paying ten bucks for a concert solo cup sized brew. I showed em my line up and setlist and you'd have thought it was the holy grail as the promoters purposefully kept that info secret(they want you inside spending money all day, not just swooping in for the headliners) and I was suddenly a hero to my new friends. I must've drank a dozen of their beers in quick succession and this liquid meal replacement on top of the accumulation of last night's alcohol, minimal sleep and spurts of jogging and adrenaline production had me in cocoon mode. I searched the grounds for a suitable hovel as people streamed into the now open event, I eventually settled on a small drainpipe jutting into a culvert. Darker and somewhat secluded I snaked myself in till only my feet dangled outside the pipe and I passed out pretty deeply for awhile. I awoke to concerned voices and some increasingly aggressive poking of my feet by a concerned concert goer. Slithering out into the midday sun I was at once again "back to the mission", and right now all I wanted to do was get inside and see live music. I circled around the sprawling complex looking for weak points in the perimeters's defenses and had all but given up when I came across a line of Port-o-potties set against the back fence on the concert side. I surmised the exposure, visualized my ascent then in one fail swoop I catapulted myself up and over the ten foot fence, on top of the potties and I hit the ground wide eyed to see that my op hadn't been detected by anyone on the other side. The familiar music and energy of the crowd buoyed me and I moshed all day and into the night around growing bonfires(they set the trash on fire) with increasingly reckless aplomb. Ever cognizant of any possible tendril of the imaginary conspiracy against me, I thought it was a good idea to burn my shoes and hobo pants in the bonfire to avoid being recognized by any of the security that had excreted me hours before. I danced and moshed barefoot for hours, even going so far as to walking on the hot coals of the fire (something I'd done at an Anthony Robbins convention when I was eighteen, the weekend before I took the State Boards for my Massage License) I finally made my way out of the show as it concluded and walked briskly away as if my security nemesis might jump out at any time (I had now convinced myself that the security guys that threw me out had also beaten me up and robbed me of my clothes and wallet... ostensibly, in my fevered mind I think so I could sue them for millions of dollars...my next 'Big Thing Mission') Barefoot and in my underwear I eventually found a construction site where I planned to spend the night. Dipping into the low sixties at night in Summer and not having fully climatized myself to these California conditions, I went about my new temporary home looking to fashion something to wear "First Blood Style". There wasn't much but I did figure out how to rip long segments of white fibrous packing material off of stacks of drywall and I set out wrapping my arms, legs and torso with these strips (for all intents and purposes I looked just like a mummy). Morning came and I started walking down the country roads (No! That god awful John Denver song better not get stuck in my head now) I found a very large all terrain truck tire cast off to the side of the road and I entertained myself by rolling it in front of me and down a hill, there was zero traffic this being dawn on a Sunday in the rural outskirts of Orange County. A lone car came rifling up behind me blaring Metallica so I shot out a hitchhikers thumb. The solo driver screeched to a halt and shouted above the Kill Em All soundtrack (It's ALL about Kill Em All, duh) ,"Hey! Were you at the concert man?!" My retort was in the affirmative in the form of a primal "WOOOOO!!" accentuated by twin devil horn hand gestures and he swung open the door. He offered me a cigarette and it was like honeydew vinewater to my senses, he shout- explained to me that he just got outta jail for a DUI incurred last night leaving the show. He was super proud somehow that he was only one of a handful of arrests made from that crowd of thousands. He dropped me outside his motel in a more suburban stretch of Irvine and excused himself as he had to go apologize to his woman. I walked over to the adjacent Denny's and was contemplating my next move when some local cops rolled up on me. The older cop chuffed intimidatingly that they had a report of me (or someone fitting my mummy-esc description) harassing people at Denny's(for once a total fabrication about me) and that I should haul ass. I started singing the "I got assaulted and robbed by the security guards at the concert" song to them and that I was trying to find a hospital as I think I had internal injuries as well. They weren't too keen but when the Big Dick talker of the two asked me in pointed Cop-eese, "Are you formally requesting medical attention to which you will be held financially responsible sir?" I said yes goddamnit, that's what the fuck I've been talking about, now do your fucking job and serve me you public servant. (The power of the victim is revealed and tolerated) The ambulance came and took me to Loma Linda University Medical Center where they gave me paper scrubs to wear and a full medical workup. I was by this time fully committed to the mission of suing the security company and had taken to using a wheel chair to make the most outta my "injuries". I lingered way too long in the ER and adjoining areas(hours) and after explaining my sob story to a hospital social worker who approached me she returned with a packet of coupons and vouchers including a cab ride to the Greyhound Bus station and a ticket back to LA. She traded me sparkly new crutches for my wheelchair and put me in the cab when it came.

It occurred to me as I waited for the bus that before I'd left Florida I had pinky promised my little sister that I would absolutely positively be at her wedding in Vegas in July. I knew it had to be somewhat close to July now and on a whim I asked the Greyhound ticket guy how far away Vegas was and when was that bus coming? Only three hours away and the Vegas bus was leaving in fifteen minutes?! Hot damn another sign.

There was a red-eye bus come in while I was waiting and when the door swung open I could hear the driver yelling in a very authoritative way and orchestrating the scene,"Y'all muthafuckas wanna scrap?! Get on out my bus and do it!" The crowd obeyed, they shuffled off the bus and I watched as they circled around two twenty something kids one black, one white and after a long bit of posturing and wanna-be gangsta talk (about just how BADASS they each thought they were) they backed down. The white boy, head on swivel still, lighting a cigarette with a shaky hand right after. Having grown up in the alcohol and instantaneously violent machismo soaked South where much much much less provocation would be a guarantee for fisticuffs, I disappointedly boarded the bus to Vegas on my newly acquired crutches. The driver didn't even care to look at my ticket (it was for LA) and off I went to Sin City.

“Bambino”-Ambrus Diossy.

8. Vegas

Far off in the mid-morning desert vista arose some carnival looking buildings. I'd never been to Vegas and the power of its mythology led me to believe that my first view of it would be a titular event akin to seeing the NYC skyline for the first time in person. We edged closer and my fever pitched anticipation got kicked in the balls- for what I was actually seeing was just the dollop of a corny little casino town named quite perfectly, "Pahrump".(Sounds like something ugly you might have to get removed from your foot) Another half hour later and I'd have the full angelic choir accompanied, ever expanding view of Vegas exposing herself to me but the false build up had taken most of the punch out of it, which turned out to be an accurate metaphor.

People and things get sun bleached in Vegas. The man-made world there is but an extension of the natural surrounding desert whose instincts are to harm you. Exposure to an environment which sucks your life-force and moisture will eventually wear anything down or in time transform it into an extension of its own vampiric self.

I was nonetheless invigorated as I felt like I was on the verge of a big windfall with the whole lawsuit thing (I was willing to settle out of court for the right price, I reckoned maybe just a million or two dollars for my trouble would suffice) I believed so fully in both the validity of this immediate mission AND in the paranoia of being surveilled by powerful forces that I continued to use my crutches as part of my act while I navigated my way around my new temporary home. I used the yellow pages and a pay phone(these were once things) to contact the personal injury attorney's office with the biggest ad, explaining to the best of my ability the ins and outs of my would be case. The man on the other end of the line seemed cautiously optimistic, but didn't exactly exude the fireworks of recognition I expected for a case of such obvious importance. I got directions to the Salvation Army Mission and crutched my ass way down, downtown past where the local Indian nation sells their tax free tobacco, past even where the haggard locals did their low rent drinking amidst newly arrived C- grade and prematurely old B-grade strippers trying to make memories and an impression good enough to warrant grinding out a greasy lap dance routine.

It would be acceptable to refer to this area as hood adjacent. Though in my experience once you've smelled and tasted the decay and predatory vibe of the older East Coast inner cities and the deep South's ghettos you kinda have to be told you're in the hood out here in the West. Trash in the gutters, a lot more pedestrians straight outta Central Casting's Mad Max files and bars on the windows of the buildings notwithstanding , the area just looked like a haphazardly erected industrial space. I passed a professional chronic street crazy who was pacing the sidewalk making a show of the schizophrenic argument he was having with himself, he was wearing what I'd estimate to be about twenty five shirts, was quarreling and cajoling amongst his voices when I walked by and locked eyes with him. I said hi and he allowed his act to fall for just a second as he recognized my own crazy, my lack of fear or derision towards him in a namaste sorta way. I later heard that his street name was "Linebacker" (the effect of all those shirts bolstering his schtick) and I couldn't help but to think that his act wasn't any different than mine, he wanted insulation, a theme and purpose.

I stuck around the Mission mostly for the next few weeks, launching mini excursions on foot deep into the Vegas Strip, orienting myself to the geography, acquiring clothes from Goodwill volunteers, even receiving a haircut (that was a thing for me once) but mostly just walking around following my intuition. Occasionally I'd talk to some random person on a bus bench and they'd take a shine to me, buy me a beer or hand me a cigarette. I'd long since shed my crutches and moved on from the "I'm gonna sue that security company" storyline and I can't even remember why. I'd sometimes make my way back to the SA Mission before check-in time and lie there in a bed even managing to sleep a bit or I'd just walk around the casinos and streets all night looking for providence to shine her light upon me. I recall during this period looking up at a large digital display on the side of a hotel on Fremont street that read the time "12:00am-Temperature- 100 degrees, and thinking that it was a wholly unnatural act to try to make a human life in this environment.

I made contact with my family and now knew that they were coming to town soon for my sister's nuptials, they all in turn were terribly concerned about my welfare but I endeavored to put their minds at ease with stories of ambitious plans I had afoot (some I even believed myself) and tried to redirect their focus upon celebrating the impending and (much more important) reason we were all here which was to witness a glorious wedding and have some fun in this place which I'd dubbed "The World's Most Elaborate Strip Mall."

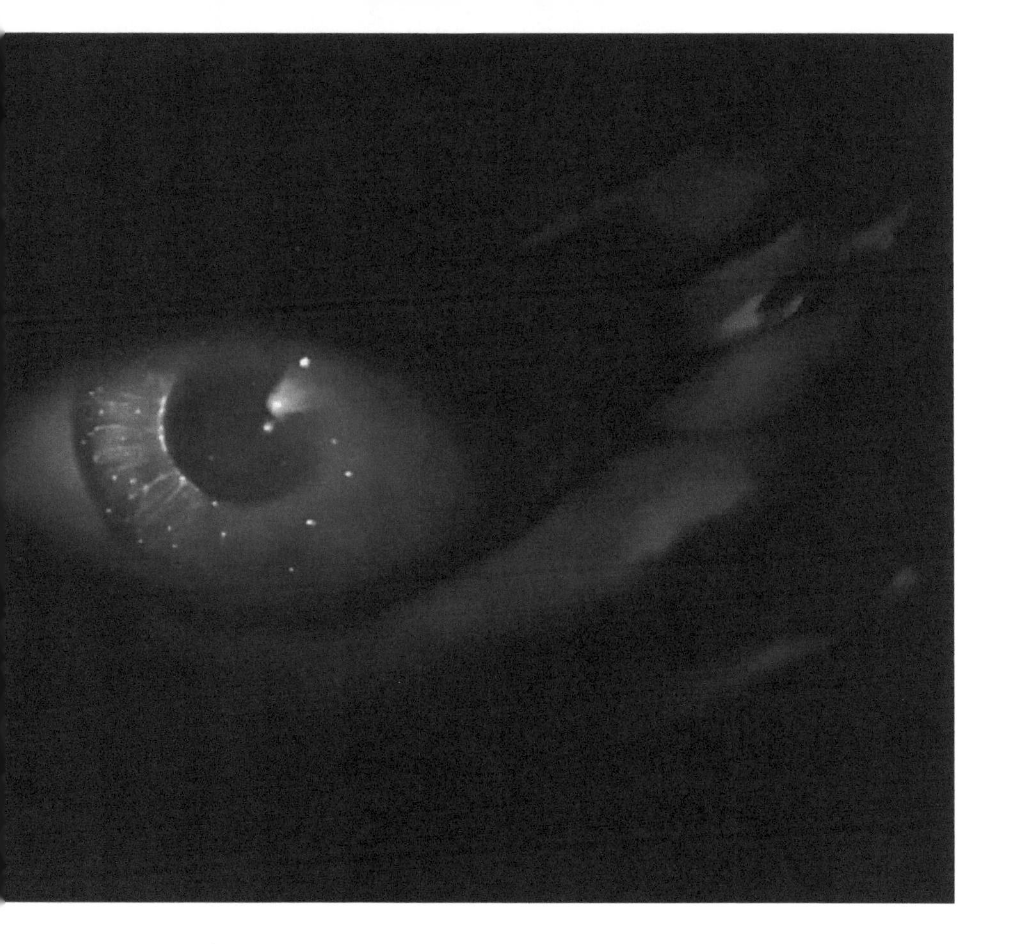

"Anastasia"- Ambrus Diossy.

9. Seattle

No matter how convincingly I thought my assurances to my family members were that I was fine, they handled me with a mixture of concern, fear and disillusionment. I did get to witness the grandeur of my sister's wedding. My erratic antics were written off and tolerated more readily by society in general while I was part of a cocktail friendly wedding party in Vegas spending lots of money. I even visited some of my old homeless buddies while still wearing the tuxedo which was rented for the occasion. My beautifully concerned family members, God love them, treated me to great meals, gave me spending money and clothes and then as a parting gift my Father even bought me a plane ticket back to Long Beach where I (kinda sorta) had a semblance of roots.

In all honesty there's a bit of obscurity in my memory of the specifics that occurred between touching down in the LBC and ending up having breakfast with my friend Chris at The Farmer's Market in Hollywood some time later. I'm sure it involved "very important" mission parameters including but not limited to; retrieving my belongings from the Hostel, being written a ticket on the subway, losing aforementioned belongings, back to staying at the mission in LB, a gifted (stolen?) bicycle, more homeless characters' drama and sneaking into and spending the night on the Paramount Lot in the New York City street block.

To his credit as a true friend, Chris showed incredible patience and restraint listening to my ramblings while buying me breakfast. He had been continuing a ferociously successful commercial voice-over run that had started in NY and he very generously paid for a Greyhound bus ticket for me to join my mother and step father up in Seattle.

The assemblage of regrets, aberrant and destructive behaviors over the past months had made somewhat of an impression upon me, but not to such a degree that it slowed my grandiose beliefs. It's difficult to execute the language proficiently here but basically I was detached from anything outside my immediate forward purview. I'd given life to so many irrational plans, theories and scenarios that I could justify everything which I had effected and affected as a necessary sacrifice to an as yet unseen goal. I believed myself to be either a misunderstood hero or a victim.

Momentum has its restraints, laws of energetic value and equations based on physical limitations. A hurricane cannot exist indefinitely but it may blow the strongest before ramping down.

I arrived in Seattle after an eternity on a Greyhound and pretty quickly gave my mother no other choice than to call the authorities to get me out of her home. She and her husband Bob had gone way way above and beyond their skill set in trying to keep me contained safely. I was running out of fuel for my bright fire but needed professional help and medication to get off this crazy train.

Risperdal was the primary anti-psychotic used on me and I named it "Rasputinal" because it reminded me of the account of all the various methods employed by the conspirators who assassinated the very energetic and vibrant mystic Rasputin. It made my body feel like it weighed seven hundred pounds and I theorized that the physical kinetic energy and momentum I had been generating by literally bouncing all around the country was finally slowed down and my mind would have no other choice but to follow.

My 5150 (Incidentally, for those who don't know, a 5150 refers to the section of the Welfare and Institutions Code which allows an adult who is experiencing a mental health crisis to be involuntarily detained for a 72- hour psychiatric hospitalization where they are evaluated to be a danger to others, or to themselves or gravely disabled) at the Snohomish County Psychiatric facility was illuminating. I met lovely imperturbable doctors who listened to me and genuinely seemed like they wanted to help. I got the opportunity to be around other patients with whom I felt a kindred connection to and educated myself further about the many factors that the medical community would state make up the function of my diagnosis which was "Bi-Polar 1", a serious chronic mental illness. They agreed to let me out after the 72hour hold. The wounds were still too fresh with Mom and Bob and I'd made such a ruckus in their apartment complex that there was no going back there so a cab picked me up and dropped me at my new home. The Everett Gospel Mission, not far from the plant where Boeing makes 747's and rolls them out of the largest moving doors in America.

A fairly Churchy incarnation of a Mission this one was, with another predicable mix of downtrodden "unlucky" men on their way to or from rock bottom and street sages who made the best of this chosen lifestyle of freedom from attachment and expectation. The food here was good and plentiful. I ironically got to taste bear meat for the first time as I'd been using the phrase "Sweet like bear meat" since I'd heard it on the show Crank Yankers years before.(It actually was kinda sweet btw). I settled into a routine of sleeping more regularly and availing myself to odd manual labor jobs that were solicited by all manner of private employers. I have a cool scar on my left fuck you finger from dropping a stump on it during a tree clearing gig and I got to participate in breaking down a ferris wheel for a traveling county fair all night in a cold light rain. (My standard line about Seattle is that the year I was there it stopped raining one time... so it could snow) I was still drinking alcohol when I could afford it and was careful not to have it detected by the staff at the Mission as that was an automatic ejection. One morning I got up and the guy who equipped you with a towel for the shower said something about the Pentagon was on fire or something. I didn't really pay it much attention till I got to the little diner we Missionites all regularly frequented and the two tv's were showing a big ass flame and smoke on one of the twin towers of the World Trade Center. My mind was trying to make sense of this and connect it to the Pentagon thing when a fuckin airplane crashed right into the second tower. Damn. Ain't that some shit.

I got picked up a bit later by a nice couple who were clearing out the overgrown yard in back of the house they'd bought that clearly used to belong to hoarders. You know what defies belief? Just how fuckin heavy an old cast iron tub that's filled with soil and has been half absorbed back into the Earth is. There were four laborers and the man who hired us all pushing the limits of our strength and leverage, sweat pouring and back muscles tearing. With the amount of effort and force given over to that task we could've picked up a mini cooper and set it on the top shelf of the cupboard. The lady was nice, she bought us all sandwiches, cokes and cigarettes for lunch and we all nervously discussed the elephant in the room of terrorist attacks but quickly got back to the business at hand.

I wish I could say that my mania had left me, but the embers of that fire still burned. And now with the synergies of impending war, the uncertainties of reprisal and enemies at the gate, the collective paranoia led me to self medicate and indulge once again into delusional thinking.

I got bounced out of the Mission. I was discovered to be drunk by a resident volunteer; a kind, intelligent man whom I'd grown to admire and have great conversations with who also happened to be a kufi wearing devout Nation of Islam Muslim. I had already let the crazy drive the vehicle again and when I was confronted for violating the sobriety policy of the house my response was to be an offensive asshole, shouting horror and ignorance at this poor man who had done absolutely nothing wrong.

I had made a little money from breaking my back wrestling that old tub and with it I got on a bus to Seattle. The dynamics of a metropolitan city are conducive to mania. The concentration of human activity and the mechanics of orchestrating all the complexities of city life necessitate an abundance of energy, which is absorbed and reflected by the senses of the maniac as stimulation. I was ramped right back up again, this time with the backdrop of a major event to add credence to any and all of my conspiratorial theories and musings. I made my way into a dive bar in a hip little downtown area. There was a thriving live music scene in Seattle still and there were a couple guys playing some original material on the tiny jazz club sized stage in the back. I looked over and saw that the large guy sitting next to me at the bar reading a newspaper was the guitarist Peter Buck from R.E.M.

This must be a sign. I engaged in ridiculous conversation with him, name dropping and referencing the cool scenes I'd been part of in the NYC world I could dredge out of my memory of time spent there. He was initially cordial, but as I overshared and overstayed my welcome he withdrew and got uncomfortable. (Sorry Peter)

I left the bar with a new mission. I had gotten close to a world famous, wealthy, talented iconic band's member and this chance encounter drew from me a response of creating a whole narrative that included me. (In my mind) I was now with the band R.E.M., promoting their arrival for a secret concert and arranging accommodations. It had the electricity of the early Beatles somehow, this completely random totally illogical story propelled me through the streets of Seattle. Emboldened by my new important position and mission, I stormed into a fancy hotel lobby and without ID or a credit card demanded celebrity treatment for my famous guest clients that were arriving soon. They had security escort me out, but instead of reaching the street I eluded them and gave spirited chase through multiple levels of parking floors and then entered the Hotel kitchens and banquet facilities where I traversed room after darkened room evading capture. The lights grew steadily closer as did the voices of the exasperated security boys as they communicated with the staccato of official first responders, which was a stretch but they technically were. I decided I'd had enough and surrendered myself and hiding spot (I'd taken off all but my underwear again), and from a prone position with my hands behind my head I proclaimed loudly that I was a psychiatric patient having a manic episode.

“Mercury” detail - Ambrus Diossy.

10. Full Stop

It was at HarborView Medical Center on Seattle's First Hill (Known to the local street people as "Pill Hill" for the facilities' multiple addiction programs and methadone clinic) that my wave of mania subsided. Whether it was the Risperdal, Lithium, Seraquil, Depakote, Klonapin and or Abilify that doused the fire or just naturally occurring adrenal fatigue, it didn't really matter, I had been jettisoned out of the storm.

I stayed in the psych ward at the hospital for three weeks. Eating and sleeping on a regular basis, getting my weight back up from the scant 150 lbs I was carried in with (I normally go around 200) and generally taking stock of my life, options and the reality of my situation. Upon release I was given a three week stay at the transitional housing wing of The Union Gospel Mission around the corner.

It took time and effort but my relationship with my mother and stepfather was salvageable and before long I was able to get a restaurant job, then a beat up little car, then a room in house somewhat near them. I was twenty-eight.

My habitual use of alcohol and my tendency to use recreational drugs as a crutch stayed with me for a few more years. It wasn't until I was given a choice between continuing to indulge in these cyclical, selfish, dangerous behaviors or lose my newly found family. Even then, it took a few more years to be completely honest with myself about my drinking and to achieve a real conscious sobriety. I don't self identify as an alcoholic or addict but I know that I'm just a better version of myself without those variables in my life.

In the subsequent years since my last manic episode I have educated myself more fully about MY condition. I can't stress enough the importance of the ownership of what that phrase means to me. My diagnosis does not define me. It gives me some guidelines of commonality with people and data that may or may not resonate with my particular experience.

I have come to believe that mania is but one of the many expressions of the same basic function. The suppression of emotional energy. When we experience trauma, anxiety, profound fear, loss, or anything which genuinely affects our emotional landscape it creates and directs emotional energy. Our body, mind, spirit combination must do something with these charged particles. In a perfect scenario the energy created is used to effect a reaction and an outcome which is beneficial- "I hear a lion roar, I get scared, I run away, I'm safe, I feel good about that and now I know about that lion." What happens when we cannot or choose not to process that experience is suppression. We stuff that emotional energy into a storage space in our consciousness. Energy cannot be destroyed, only channeled or transformed. So you may find temporary ways to expand your storage area or try to repair the leaks in it but that energy is still there and if you're taking further steps to avoid dealing with your issues(self medicating), those steps in turn just create more and more energy until it manifests in some way. For me it was mania but that energetic volume could've become; PTSD, substance/work/ sex or gambling addictions, depression, anxiety, physical disease, obsessive compulsion, eating disorder, schizophrenia, sociopathic tendencies, etc.

I found that I can maintain balance and still remain true to who I am. For me that feat has everything to do with finding a partner that will not tolerate anything but complete truth and accountability. Like anything of value, balance and happiness take constant conscious work and maintenance. The more difficult the work- the more honest the appraisal- the straighter the path is to acceptance. I'm humbled by the love shown to me by those who did not write me off. I revel in the strides I've made to forgive the people and situations which gave me hardships (especially myself.)

We are the accumulation of the choices we have made regardless of the reasons we use to justify those decisions. This responsibility binds us to the outcomes be it glory or disappointment. We are all a work in progress and have infinite possibilities and eventualities. You are beautiful and you deserve to love the ride you're on.

Kalvin Seth Brubaker

Arithmophobic polymath aphorist. Loves naps, metal, cinema, edged weapons, ice baths, spicy chili peppers, obstacle course racing, cooking and acting. Lives in Los Angeles where he serves his dogs and family at their pleasure. Been mania free for 19 years and counting.

Back Cover- "The Mean and the Splendid"-Ambrus Diossy.

CPSIA information can be obtained
at www.ICGtesting.com
Printed in the USA
LVHW070023231220
674885LV00001B/9

* 9 7 8 0 5 7 8 7 6 9 2 0 2 *